Amanda's First Visit to the Dentist

By: Angelica Almeida Corcoran

Illustrated by: Nabeel Tahir

Dedication

To my beloved children, Amanda and Kj,
whose laughter and curiosity inspire every page.
May you always dream big, explore boldly, and,
most importantly, always be yourselves.
Know that you are deeply loved.

Mom

"Good morning, sunshine! Are you ready for your dentist appointment?" asked Mom.
"Yes!" said Amanda.

"Okay, Amanda, go brush your teeth," said Mom.
"Make sure to brush all of them. I'm coming to check!"

"Amanda, today you're going to see the dentist and the dental hygienist. The hygienist's name is Angelica, and the dentist's name is Dr. Lollipop. They are very nice!"

"What are they going to do, Mommy?" asked Amanda.
"The dental hygienist will count all your teeth and make
sure they're squeaky clean," Mom explained. "Angelica
will also take pictures of your teeth."

"What about the dentist?" asked Amanda.
"Dr. Lollipop will check to make sure you don't have any cavities,"
said Mom. "He uses a special tool called an explorer to make sure
every tooth is healthy."

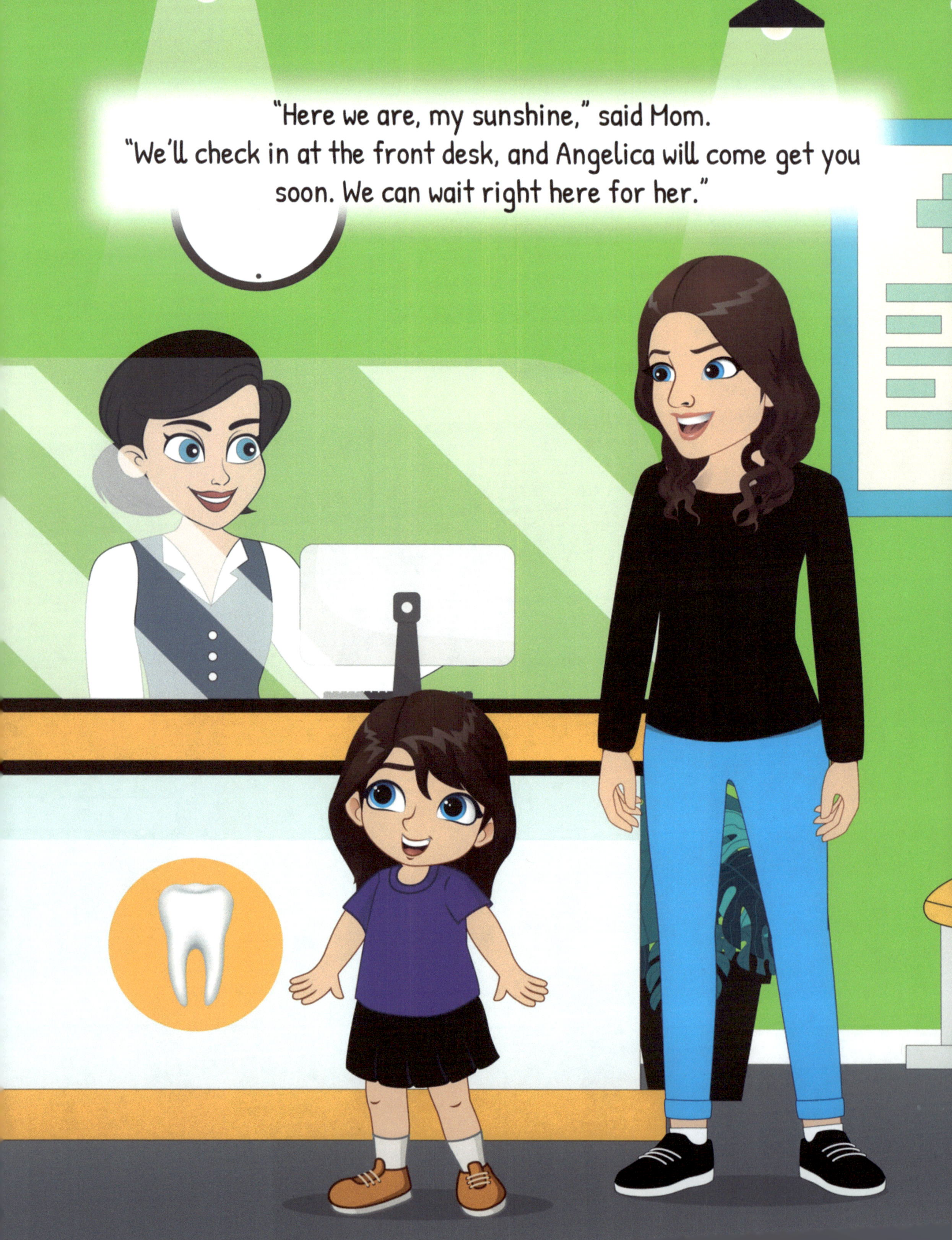

"Here we are, my sunshine," said Mom.
"We'll check in at the front desk, and Angelica will come get you soon. We can wait right here for her."

Angelica has super cool tools! Her fun chair goes up and down and backward, so she can see all of your teeth. She has a tiny mirror to look inside your mouth and a little helper named Mr. Thirsty who gently sucks up all your saliva.

"Hi, Amanda!" said Angelica, the hygienist.
"Do you want to come see my cool room? I have lots of things to show you."

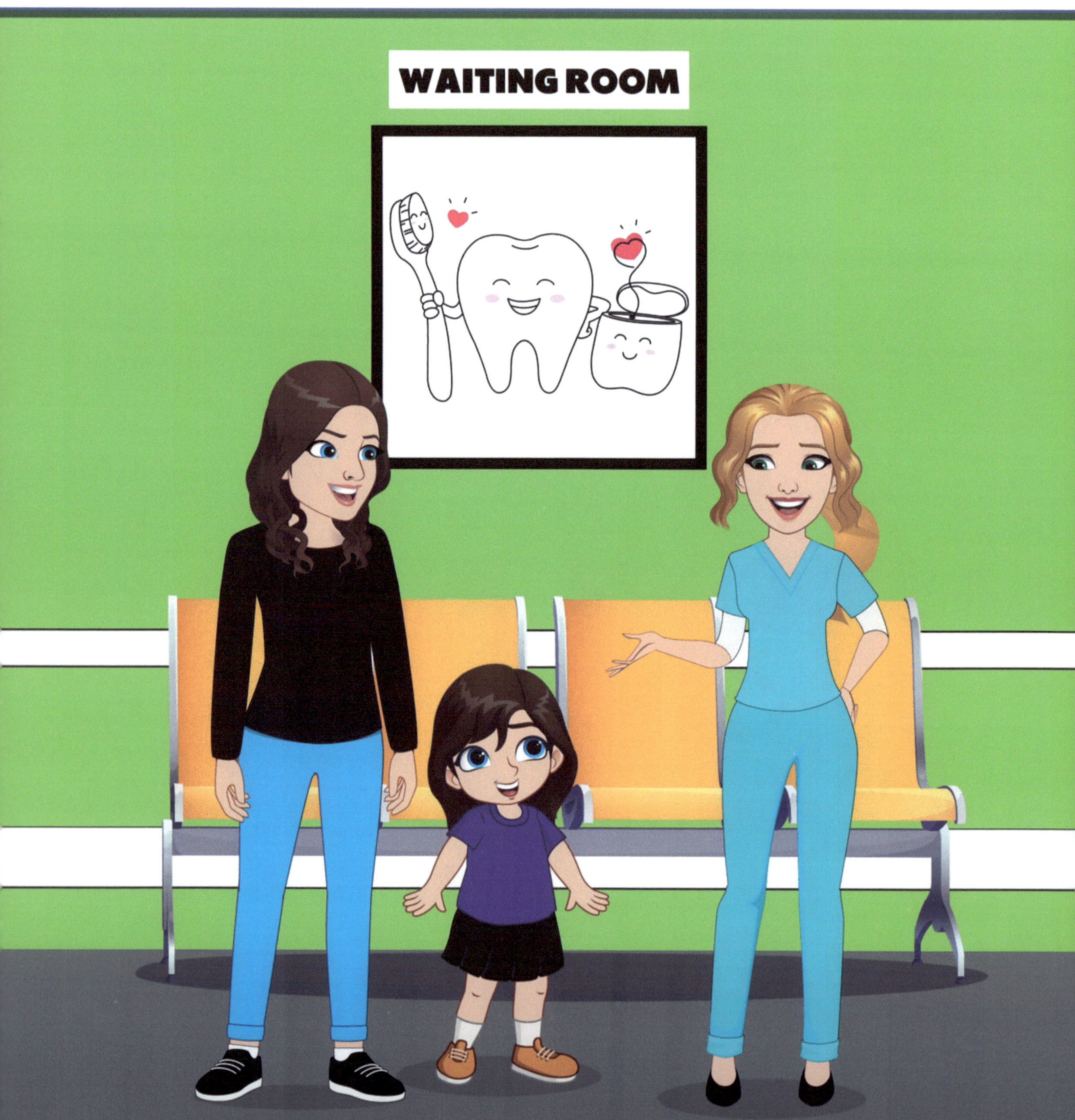

"Amanda, first I'm going to count your teeth," said Angelica. "Then I'll clean them with my special toothbrush and toothpaste to make them shiny. I'll also use my explorer to check your teeth and my tools to remove any plaque."

"What's plaque?" asked Amanda.
"I'm glad you asked!" said Angelica. "Plaque is sticky goo that builds up on teeth if we don't brush them. If it stays too long, it can cause cavities. Brushing and flossing keep our teeth clean and happy!"

"Sometimes we take pictures of your teeth with a special camera called X-rays," said Angelica.
"Do I have to say cheeeeese?" asked Amanda.
Angelica smiled. "Not for this one, Amanda."

"This camera is extra special," said Angelica. "It can see your teeth and bones—even the parts under your gums!"
"That's so cool!" said Amanda with excitement.

"Amanda, you can sit in my cool chair now," said Angelica. "I'm going to put this bib on you so you don't get toothpaste on your pretty outfit." "Okay!" said Amanda.
As the chair went down, Amanda giggled. "This chair is fun!"

"Amanda, guess how many teeth you have?" asked Angelica.
"I don't know!"
"You have 20 teeth, and it looks like you're doing a great job brushing them! Good job, Amanda!"

"Amanda, Dr. Lollipop will come in now to check your teeth, okay?"
"Hello, Amanda, I'm Dr. Lollipop," said the dentist. "I'm going to use my special explorer to check for cavities, alright?"
"Sure!" said Amanda.

"Dr. Lollipop, how do you fix cavities?" asked Amanda.
"I have another special tool called Mr. Highspeed," he explained.
"He's very fast and makes a little noise. When I clean out a
cavity, we fill the tooth with a super cool material so it becomes
healthy again." "Wow! That's awesome!" said Amanda.

"Amanda, at the end of your visit, you can pick a prize from our treasure box! You did such a great job today!"
"Thank you!" said Amanda. "Can I pick one for my brother Kj?"
"Of course!" said Angelica.

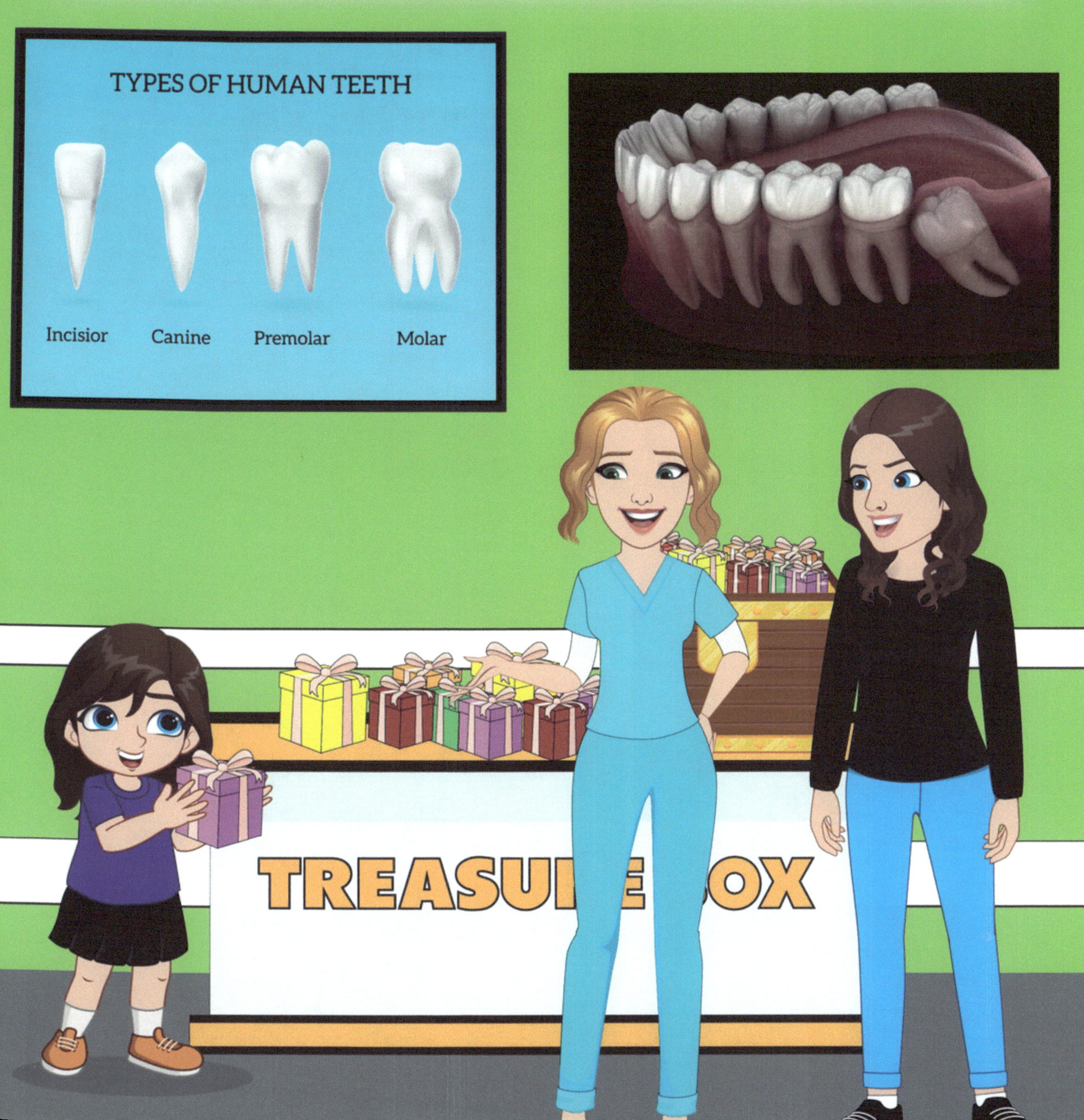

"Mommy! Mommy! Now I can tell Kj all about the dentist visit! Can I come with him when it's his turn?"
"Yes," said Mom. "But Kj is still a baby. When it's his turn, you can come help him."

"It was very nice of you to pick a toy for your brother," said Mom. "I'm proud of you!"

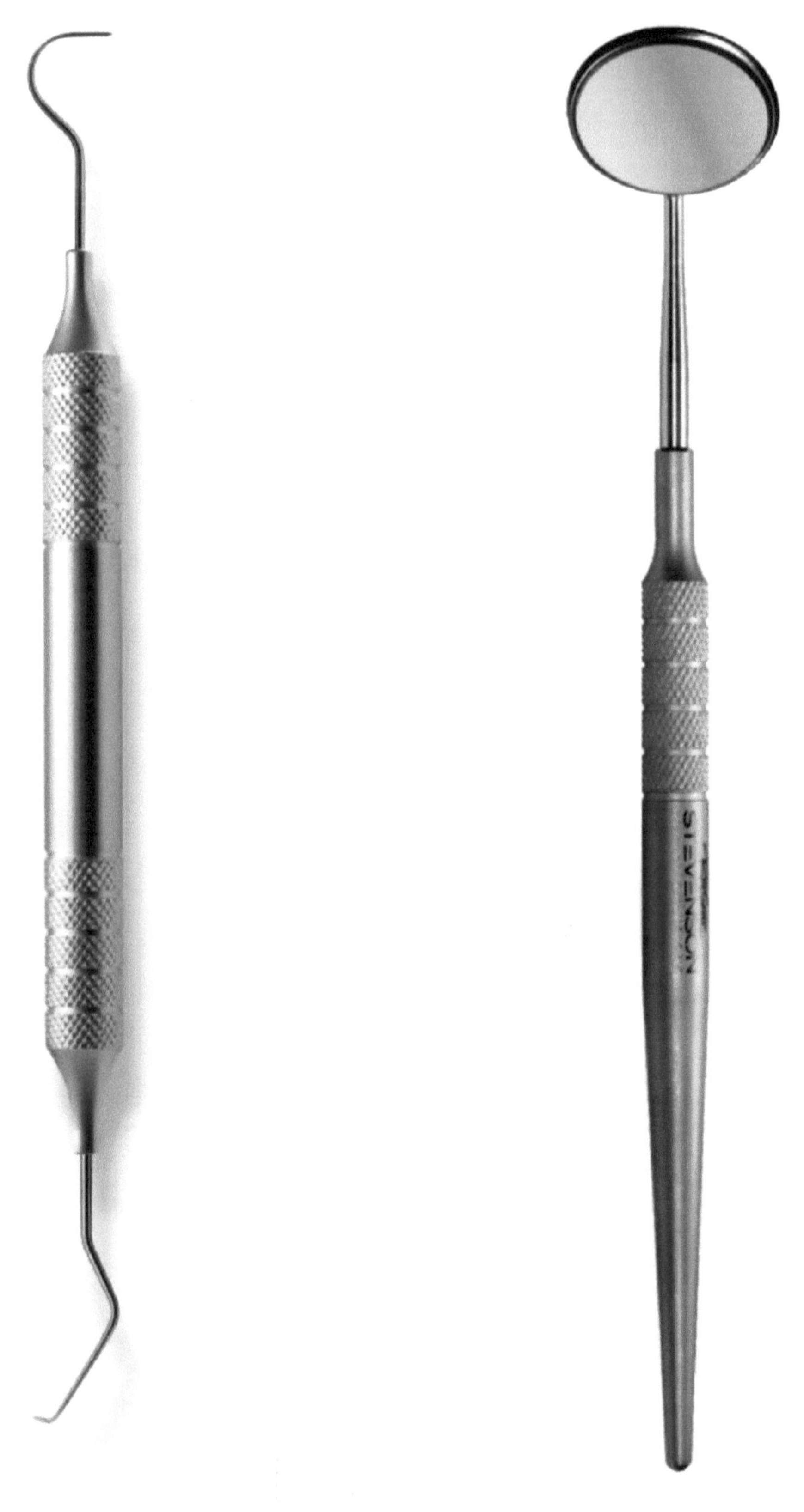

Explorer/ Probe

Mouth Mirror

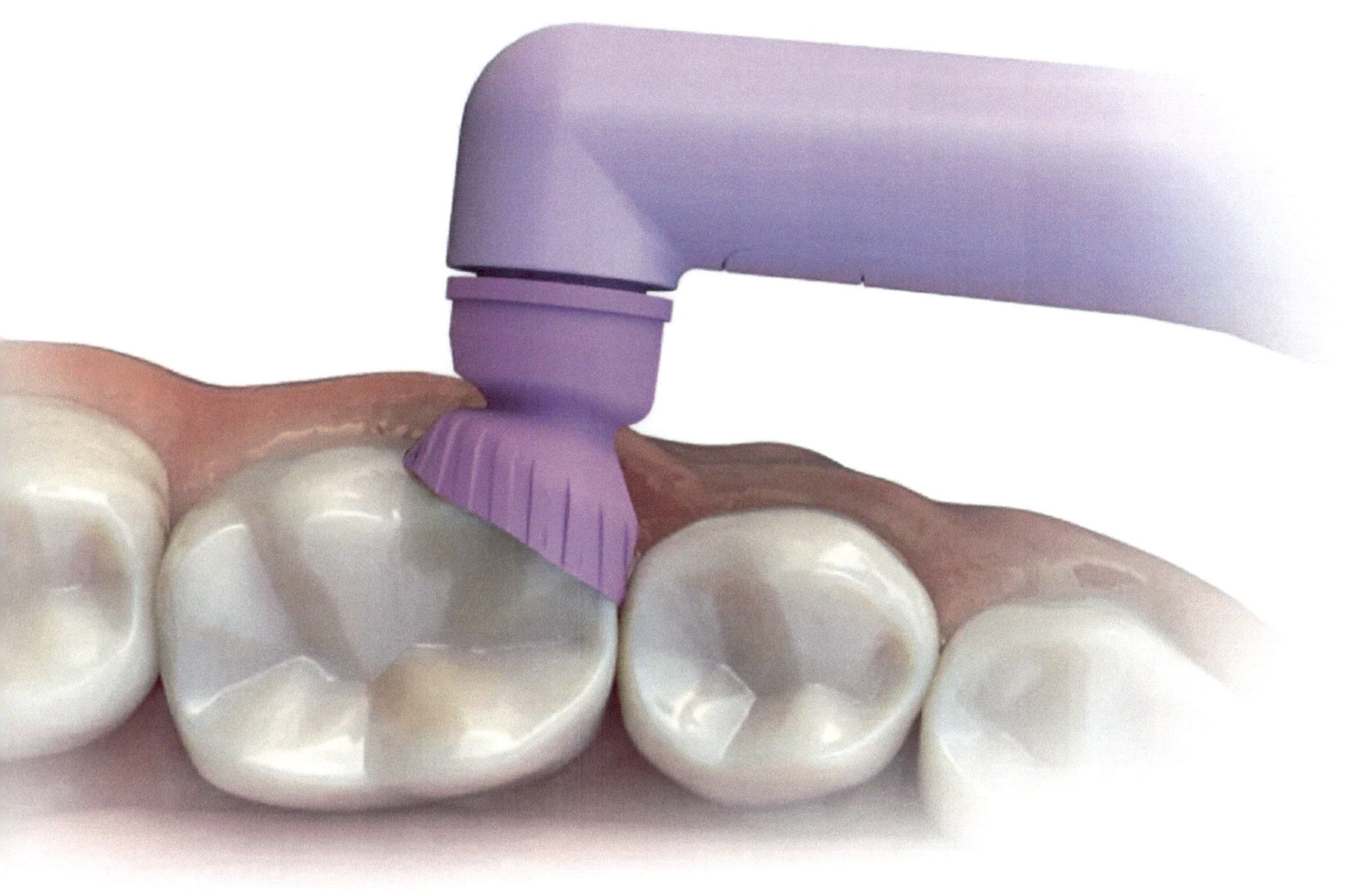

ProFlare Articulating Disposable Prophy Angle

Structure of
The Healthy Tooth

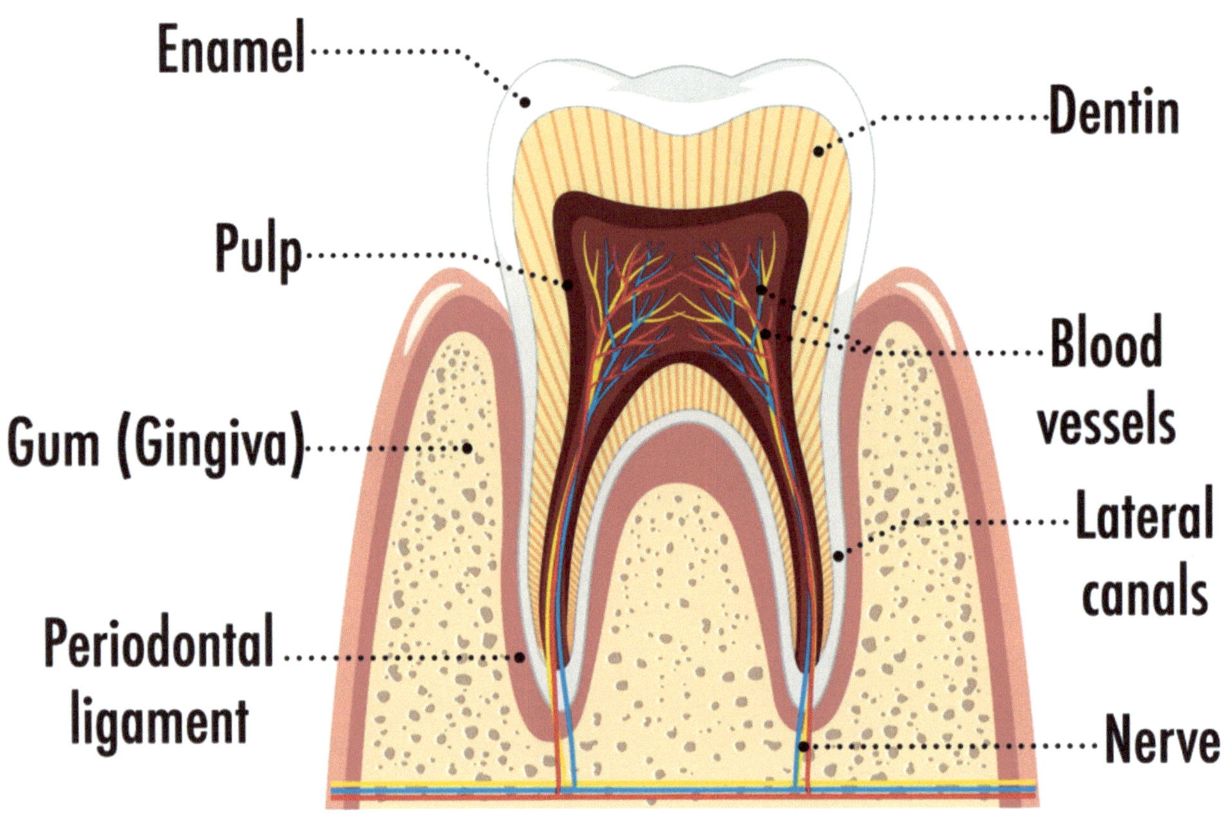

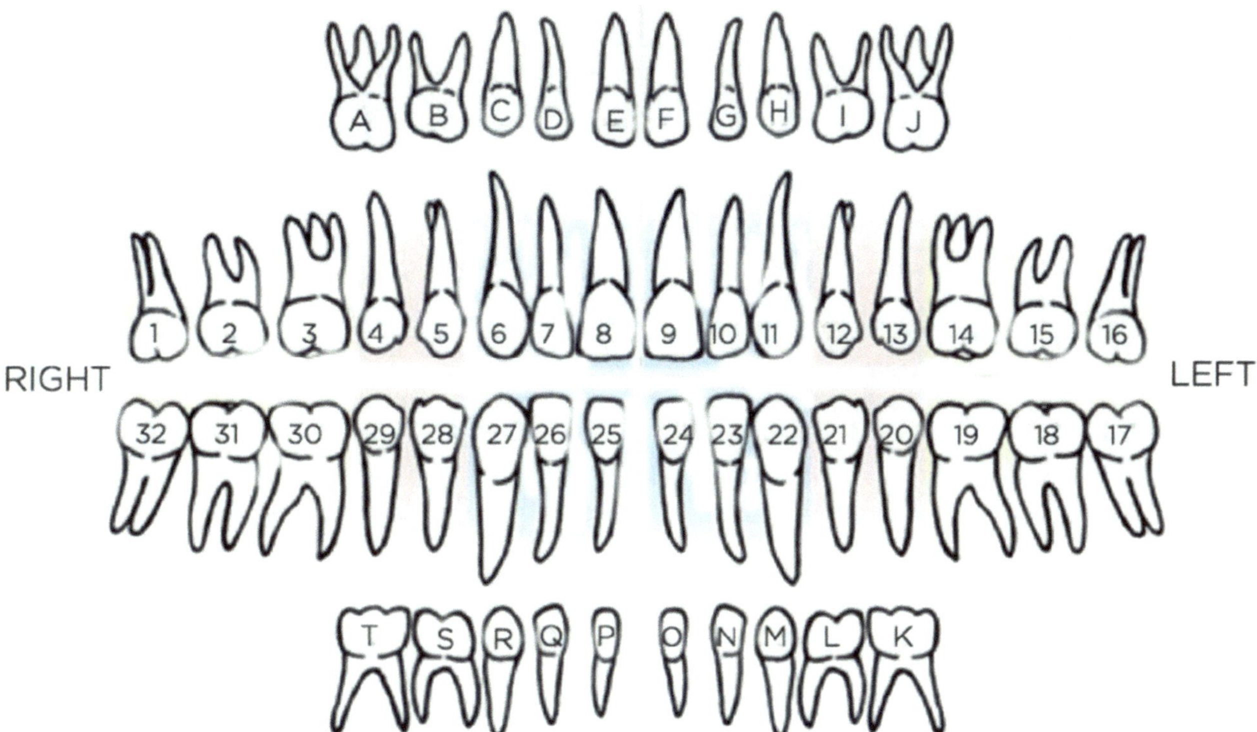

A B C D E F G H I J
1 2 3 4 5 6 7 8 9 10 11 12 13 14 15 16
RIGHT
LEFT
32 31 30 29 28 27 26 25 24 23 22 21 20 19 18 17
T S R Q P O N M L K

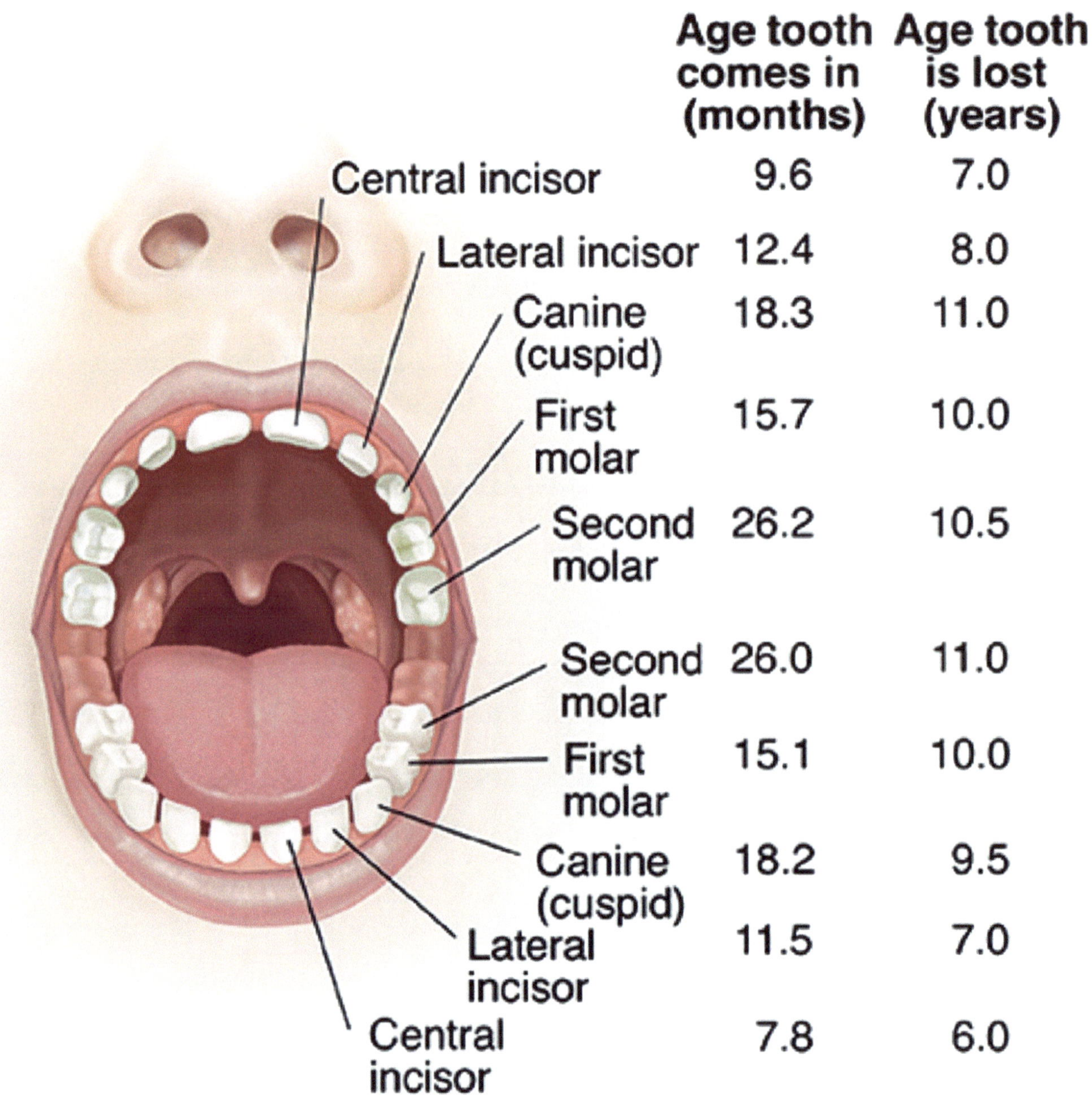

Age tooth comes in (months)
Age tooth is lost (years)
Central incisor
9.6
7.0
Lateral incisor
12.4
8.0
Canine (cuspid)
18.3
11.0
First molar
15.7
10.0
Second molar
26.2
10.5
Second molar
26.0
11.0
First molar
15.1
10.0
Canine (cuspid)
18.2
9.5
Lateral incisor
11.5
7.0
Central incisor
7.8
6.0

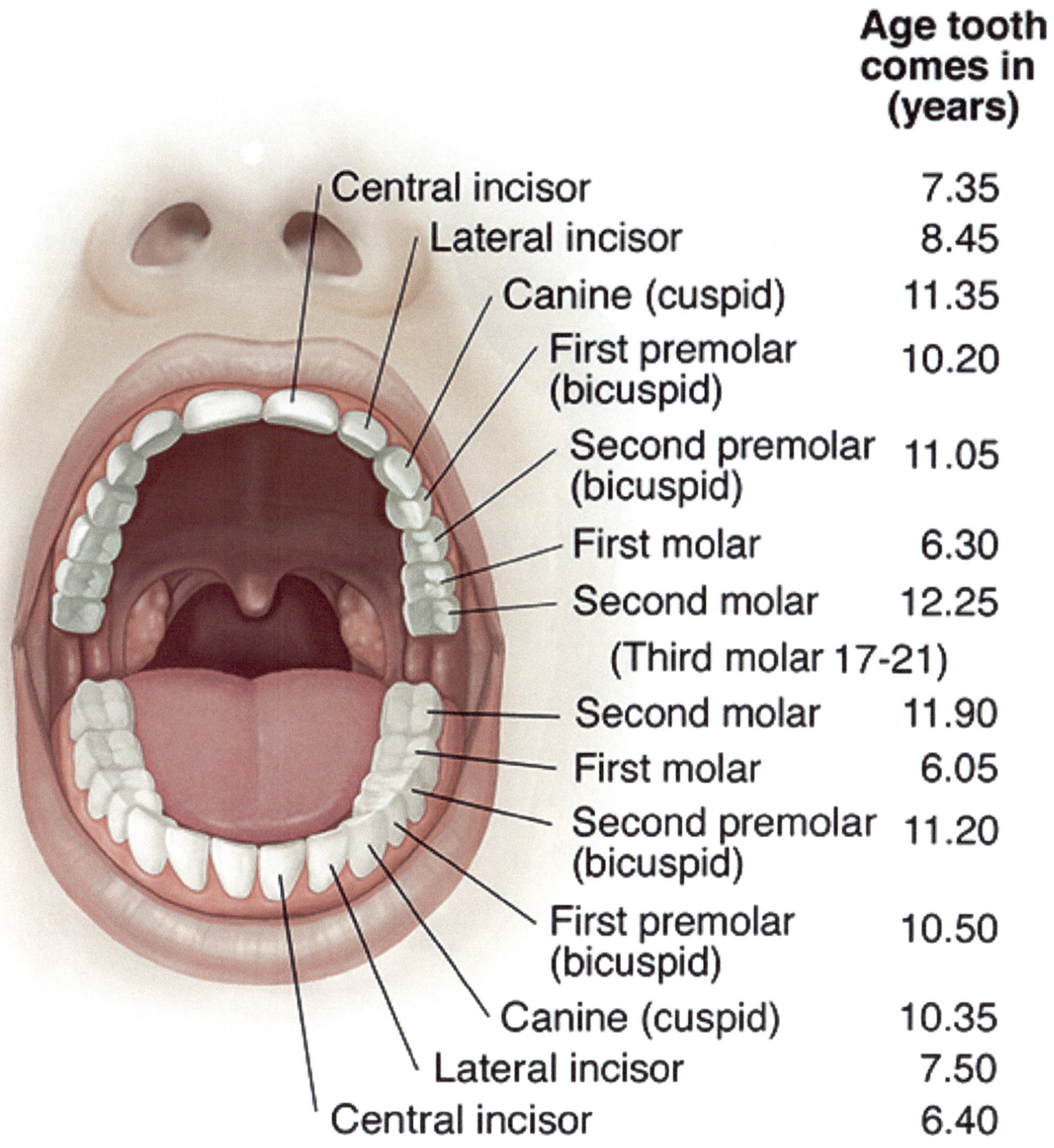

Age tooth comes in (years)
Central incisor 7.35
Lateral incisor 8.45
Canine (cuspid) 11.35
First premolar (bicuspid) 10.20
Second premolar (bicuspid) 11.05
First molar 6.30
Second molar 12.25
(Third molar 17-21)
Second molar 11.90
First molar 6.05
Second premolar (bicuspid) 11.20
First premolar (bicuspid) 10.50
Canine (cuspid) 10.35
Lateral incisor 7.50
Central incisor 6.40

ACKNOWLEDGMENTS

To all my beloved nephews and nieces, and to my family - your love, strength and presence mean more to me than words can say.
To my wonderful nephews — Nicholas Garcia and Benjamin Garcia, who once believed I was the Tooth Fairy — thank you for filling my life with magic, laughter, and imagination.
And to Jacob Almeida and Samuel Almeida, whose curiosity and joy brighten every room. Thank you for inspiring stories like this one.
You all remind me that childhood is full of wonder, and I'm grateful to share a part of that with you.